# EltonJohn

| | |
|---|---|
| text | **Paula Taylor** |
| illustrations | **John Keely** |
| design concept | **Mark Landkamer** |

published by    **Creative Education**
**Mankato, Minnesota**

Published by Creative Educational Society, Inc.,
123 South Broad Street, Mankato, Minnesota 56001
Copyright © 1975 by Creative Educational Society, Inc. International
copyrights reserved in all countries.
No part of this book may be reproduced in any form without written permission
from the publisher. Printed in the United States.
Distributed by Childrens Press, 1224 West Van Buren Street, Chicago, Illinois 60607

Library of Congress Numbers: 75-23084   ISBN: 0-87191-457-3

Library of Congress Cataloging in Publication Data
Taylor, Paula.     Elton John.
SUMMARY: A biography of the English rock star famous for his
frenzied performances of his own compositions.
1. John, Elton—Juvenile literature.   (1. John, Elton. 2. Musicians)
I. Keely, John.   II. Title.
ML3930.J58T4   784'.092'4 (B)   75-23084   ISBN 0-87191-457-3

Slowly, the lights dim. "And now, ladies and gentle-men," a voice says, "this evening's hostess. . ." A huge backdrop, picturing Elton John, is pulled aside. A single spotlight on stage focuses on a gleaming staircase and five brightly colored pianos. The hostess, dressed in a low-cut, sequinned gown, steps from the shadows toward the microphone.

"Hi," she purrs. "I'd like to introduce some of tonight's guests — very important people from around the world who wouldn't have dared miss this gala evening." Down the staircase, one after another, leap nine figures, portraying the Queen of England, Elvis Presley, Franken-stein, the Pope, the Beatles, Batman and Robin, Groucho Marx, and Mae West. Slowly, the celebrities raise the covers of the five pianos. Huge, inlaid letters appear, spelling E-L-T-O-N. Out of the pianos, flutters a flock of doves.

The audience cheers wildly. What will Elton think of next? And what will he be wearing this time? His silver Uncle Sam outfit and orange goggles? His sunglasses with battery-powered windshield wipers? As the doves fly about overhead, the hostess introduces the members of the band. But the audience isn't paying much attention. Everyone is staring expectantly toward the wings, waiting for Elton John to appear.

Finally, the hostess pauses. "Here he is, the *biggest, largest,* most *gigantic* and *fantastic* man . . . ELTON JOHN!" A glittering figure emerges from the shadows. Resplendent in a silver lamé jump suit trimmed with white ostrich feathers, Elton peers mischievously at the audi-ence from behind huge, white-rimmed glasses.

As the roar of applause hits him, Elton grins and waves to the audience. Balancing on tall, silver platform shoes, he walks slowly over to the grand piano and sits down, looking tiny against its huge bulk. For a moment, he hesitates. Then he nods to the band. Down come his fingers on the keys, pounding out the sounds of "Elderberry Wine."

Elton hunches over the keyboard, concentrating on his music. During difficult passages, he grimaces, gritting his teeth and puckering up his face. Solemnly, he sings two wistfully romantic numbers, "Your Song" and "High Flying Bird." Then comes a fast number. Gradually, the pace of the songs picks up.

With "Hercules," something snaps. The solemn pianist becomes a whirling dervish. Elton kicks away the piano stool. His stubby fingers still punching out the chords, he twists his body into deep knee bends and back bends. He even does a handstand on the keys. Alternating blue, red, yellow, and silver lights bathe his frenzied form in eerie waves of color.

Finally, Elton spins away from the piano. Without missing a beat, he boogies across the stage, clapping in time to the music. Behind him, the band is keeping up the feverish tempo. Waves of sound swell higher and higher. Encouraged by the wildly-cheering crowd, Elton leans down over the edge of the stage to shake some of the hands stretched out to him. As a grand finale, he leaps onto the piano. Triumphantly, he acknowledges the deafening applause. He seems larger than life — the Hercules of the Rock World.

After the show, the fans scramble briefly for free Elton John tee shirts. Then, slowly, the huge amphitheater empties. Backstage, the band members pack up their instruments. Sound men roll up wires and check speakers and amplifiers. A costumer examines Elton's silver jump

suit; some of the seams may need to be sewn up.

Off in a corner, a short, stocky young man in jeans and a sweat shirt sits alone, observing all the commotion from behind dark glasses. Stripped of his glittering costume, Elton John looks quite ordinary. He would be easy to miss in a crowd.

But several fans who've sneaked past security guards recognize him. They hold out copies of his records for him to sign. "Fantastic show," says one fan.

"Your albums are *far out!*" adds another enthusiastically.

"Thank you," replies Elton, not knowing what else to say. Embarrassed, he looks down; and his face goes red. As the fans walk away, Elton continues sitting silently and staring into space.

# The Real Elton

"My private life is very quiet," says Elton John. "I'm not on any rock star sort of circuit . . . I'm not involved in any of the supposedly hip things — I don't use drugs, don't even smoke, and I'm giving up alcohol." Elton associates mainly with a small group of close friends. He hates going to parties. When he has to attend a show business gala, he can usually be found alone in a corner, sipping a coke. "I don't mix much," he explains.

On his rare days off, Elton prefers staying at home. He owns a luxurious bachelor pad, "Chez Hercules," hidden away on the wooded grounds of a former estate, west of London. The house reflects Elton's passion for neatness. From the carefully-kept grounds to the tastefully-lighted art objects and the precisely-folded towels in the marble bathroom, everything is in its place.

Only a few bizarre touches hint at the outrageous side of Elton John. In the front yard is a huge stone, almost like a tombstone. Large letters carved on it spell out HER- CULES. Just inside the front door lurks a life-sized toy panda bear. A gleaming suit of armor guards the stairway.

Records are everywhere. Elton owns 5,000 Lp's, 2,500 45's, and 800 tapes. Most of them are in piles underfoot, the only untidy aspect of the place. Elton says he can't find the records he's looking for when they're put away on a shelf. When he thinks of a song, he likes to be able to pick out a record instantly. At home, he listens to records, usually those of the newest rock groups much of the time. But he doesn't play the piano much — just doodles occasionally.

Offstage, Elton prefers not to be noticed. The first time he came to the United States, his P.R. man thought up a flashy gimmick to introduce the new British singer to American audiences. Elton John and his entourage were met at the Los Angeles airport by a bright red British double-decker bus with a huge sign announcing, "ELTON JOHN HAS ARRIVED." When Elton saw it, he turned almost as red as the bus. He and his band rode the bus through the streets of Los Angeles, crouched down in their seats so no one would see them.

Elton still blushes when he remembers riding on that garish bus. Yet he thinks nothing of jumping around on stage in yellow overalls, a top hat, and white sneakers with wings on the heels. Which is the real Elton John — the shy loner or the exuberant clown? Probably both. Elton says his quiet and his outrageous selves exist side by side. When he dresses up in wild clothes and walks out on stage, his whole personality changes.

After his first hit record, *Elton John,* people began

flocking to his concerts to hear him in person. Most of them expected to see an intense, moody figure like the one pictured on the Elton John record jacket. It tickled Elton to see their surprise when he appeared in purple tights and kicked over the piano stool.

"I want to be the complete opposite of what people want me to be," he says stubbornly. "I couldn't sit at the piano every night and just play soft songs. I'd get bored to bloody tears. It's not me. . . . My music can be very quiet. But I just like to get up there and tear my hair out. I'm really, basically, just a rock 'n roll freak."

## Alias Reg Dwight

In his zany stage act, Elton John may be making up for all the fun he missed as a child. He wasn't Elton John then. His name was Reginald Kenneth Dwight, and he lived in a sedate London suburb. The Dwight family led a comfortable, ordinary life, much like their well-to-do neighbors. Reggie was sent to a private school, where he was a good student. His parents expected him to go on to the university.

But Reggie Dwight's life was not as idyllic as it might have seemed to an outsider. He didn't get along well with his father, a squadron leader in the Royal Air Force. To his son, Mr. Dwight seemed snobbish and rather cold. "He never let me do anything that I wanted," Reg remembered later. "I couldn't even play in the garden, in case I might damage his rose beds. I was petrified of him. My mother was everything to me, marvelous; but I used to pray that father wouldn't come home at the weekends."

13

Reggie and his father often argued. The subject about which they disagreed most strongly was music. Reggie had shown a talent for music at an early age, picking out tunes on the piano when he was only three. At nine, he started formal piano lessons; and when he was 12, he won a part-time scholarship to the famous Royal Academy of Music.

By that time, American rock 'n roll was taking England by storm. Mr. Dwight thought the new music was awful, and Reggie was forbidden to listen to it. But Reg found the insistent beat of rock 'n roll irresistible. He bought record after record, playing them when his father was away.

Reggie admired Bill Haley and Elvis Presley; but his real hero was Jerry Lee Lewis, the frenzied piano player. When no one was around, Reggie would pretend he was Lewis. He'd stamp his feet and bang the piano furiously, his hair hanging down and his arms flailing the air.

Reggie played the piano constantly, experimenting with the popular tunes. As time went on, he played classical music less and less. His mother was not terribly concerned that Reggie wasn't practicing the pieces his piano teacher assigned. Mrs. Dwight was convinced that her son was a genius. She marveled at the way he could play any melody perfectly the first time he heard it. Besides, she liked rock and roll music herself. But Mr. Dwight took a dim view of his wife's encouraging Reggie's "low class" musical tastes. "He's got to get this pop nonsense out of his head," Mr. Dwight insisted.

Reggie became increasingly unhappy. He hated upsetting his father, but he didn't like playing classical music. When he played a Beethoven sonata, he had to play the way someone else wanted him to. The notes were written down, and his teacher told him the way the piece should sound. When he played "Rock Around the Clock," he was free to experiment and improvise. There was no right or wrong way to play it, and the piece came out differently every time. He felt as though he were creating the music himself.

Even though he wanted to please his father, Reggie couldn't give up playing popular music. He started skipping his piano lessons, riding on the subway for hours, rather than getting off at the Royal Academy of Music.

When Reg was 14, his parents were divorced. More uncertain and unhappy than ever, Reg found comfort in food. He grew pudgy, then definitely overweight. Being fat made him even more miserable. At school, he studied less and less, barely making it through his exams. He spent hours lying on his bed, imagining himself on stage, singing like Elvis. He was determined to get into the glamorous world of show business and become a rock 'n roll star.

# Blues-ology

Unlike most fat, lonely kids who dream of becoming superstars, Reg Dwight finally did become a part of the glittering world he dreamed of. But success came many years after Reg got his start as a member of an unknown band.

In 1961, when he was 14, Reg and some of his friends began holding informal jam sessions at school. At first, the group included only bass, piano, and drums. Later, they added a sax, a trumpet, and a guitar. The band, which they called Bluesology, often played at youth club dances.

To get enough money to buy an electric piano and

amplifiers, Reg got a weekend job at the pub in a nearby hotel. He could play anything the customers asked for. Soon the pub was packed on Friday and Saturday nights, and Reg was earning $75 a week.

In 1964, when he was 17, Reg managed to scrape through his A-level exams (roughly equivalent to an American high school diploma). He left school and got a job as a "tea boy" in a record store. Besides making tea and serving it to everyone who worked in the store, he had to wrap parcels and take them to the post office several times a day.

Meanwhile, Bluesology was building a modest reputation in the outlying districts of London. Reg said later that Bluesology never really clicked because they were always one step behind everyone else. As a joke, they purposely played obscure numbers few people had ever heard of. One night the band was given an ultimatum by a gang of tough motorcycle riders in the audience: either they played hit songs or their gear would be smashed. After that, they played fewer unusual numbers.

Occasionally, the group went on tour, doing 9 or 10 shows a week, their equipment crammed in the back of their small Ford van. The pace was hectic. They'd do a show in London at 4:30 p.m., drive 150 miles to Birmingham and do a "double," and then drive back to London and play a club at 4:30 in the morning. There was no manager to handle their gear, and the van was always breaking down.

In 1965, a year after Elton had left school, Bluesology turned professional. They got jobs backing visiting American acts like Patti LaBelle and Stevie Wonder. As they became better known, Bluesology began getting bookings at prestigious London clubs. At a club called the Crom-

wellian, they met Long John Baldry, a British blues singer. Baldry asked the group to back him.

With Bluesology, Long John Baldry had a hit record, "Let the Heartaches Begin." By that time, the group included some first-rate musicians, but the star was John Baldry. Everywhere they played, Baldry would do his hit number, and everyone in the audience would scream.

The other members of the band were satisfied with their modest success. But with every performance, Reg became more bored and frustrated. He wanted to do more than play the piano for someone else — he wanted to be a star. But he was beginning to realize he'd never be more than a back-up musician with Bluesology.

When the group was booked for a cabaret tour, Reg decided he couldn't put off leaving any longer. He simply couldn't face playing to people who were clanking knives and forks, instead of listening to the music. "There are so many good people going around in bands who are afraid to take the plunge or don't get the chance," Reg said later. "The only reason I did was that I was so depressed and miserable I just had to."

# Enter Bernie Taupin

Reg started looking around for another job. One day he saw an ad in a newspaper:

LIBERTY RECORDS
WANTS TALENT
Artistes/ /Composers
Singer-Musicians
To Form New Group

Reg quickly made an appointment for an audition.

When he arrived at the Liberty sound studios, Reg told the people in charge that he could write songs — but not lyrics. "Can you sing?" they asked. "Of *course,* I can sing," he replied confidently. But since he'd never sung with Bluesology, the only numbers he could remember were the ones he'd sung four years before at the pub in the Northwood Hills Hotel.

Before he finished the first song, Reg knew the verdict. "Sorry," said the Liberty representatives. "No chance here."

But as Reg was going out the door, one of the men stopped him. "We've got some lyrics here from a guy in Lincolnshire named Bernie Taupin," he said, "We can't use his stuff, but maybe you could take a look at it."

"Thanks," mumbled Reg. His face still red with embarrassment, he shoved the papers in his pocket and hurried out of the studio.

When he got home, Reg began studying the sheets of paper the man had given him. As he read through the lyrics, something clicked. He sat down at the piano and quickly wrote out melodies to most of Bernie Taupin's lyrics. As he wrote, he had an eerie feeling that it was the "start of something."

Reg and Bernie began corresponding. More sheets of poetry arrived from Lincolnshire. Bernie's lyrics were rarely in verse form and were sometimes as many as 115 lines long. Studying them, Reg wondered, "Where do I start?" The poems were crammed with fantastic images. Bernie wrote about love and loneliness, freedom and violence, death and mystery. But whatever the subject, Reg was able to capture the poem's mood perfectly in his music.

Before they met, Reg and Bernie had written over 20 songs together by mail. Reg was anxious to try out the new songs in a sound studio, but he didn't have the money to pay for a lot of demos.

Then one of his friends told him about the Dick James Music Company which was becoming very liberal with their sound studio. Reg found it was possible for almost anyone to walk in and record. So he began making regular trips to the James studios to make demos of the new songs.

One day while he was recording, a small, dark-haired young man walked into the studio and sat down in a corner. When the session ended, Reg went over to him. "Who are you?" he asked.

"Bernie Taupin," the stranger replied.

"Oh . . ." said Reg awkwardly. "Hello." Having met at last, the two went off to a hamburger grill around the corner to have coffee.

For months after that, Reg continued to cut demos. Meanwhile, he earned a meagre living clerking in a record store and playing occasionally with Bluesology. After he'd recorded 50 or 60 songs, there was a sudden change of policy at James Music. Dick James had discovered that a lot of groups were using his studio without paying. He ordered all the freeloaders out.

But one of the engineers went to Dick James and pleaded with him to let Reg and Bernie stay. After hearing some of their demos, James signed them to a contract at $30 a week each. Reg was delighted. At last he could leave Bluesology for good and get off the road.

But after a few months with Dick James Music, Reg was almost as miserable as he'd been with Bluesology. James wanted him and Bernie to write Top Forty songs for currently popular musicians. For almost a year, they tried. They turned out song after song. But none of the numbers sold, and Dick James began getting impatient.

Then a song-plugger named Steve Brown suggested that they stop trying to write hit songs and write what they wanted to. The result was "Lady Samantha," which, ironically enough, became a hit. "From that point on," Elton says, "we've never written a song that we haven't liked."

# The Transformation

After signing the contract with Dick James Music in 1969, Reg played one last date with Bluesology. On the plane back to London, he decided to change his name. "Reginald Kenneth Dwight," he mused aloud to his friends. ". . . it sounds like the guy who cleans the windows. If I ever do get a record out, it couldn't possibly be a hit with a name like 'Reg Dwight' on it."

The group tossed around a number of names. The one Reg liked best was Elton, the name of Bluesology's alto sax man, Elton Dean. But he couldn't take over Dean's whole name. Reg glanced around the plane. His friend John Baldry was sitting several seats back. That was it — Elton *John*. Nobody actually liked it, Reg admitted later; but they couldn't think of anything better.

So Reg Dwight became Elton John. With his new name, he seemed to acquire a whole new personality. He became more outgoing and confident. He worried less about doing what other people wanted him to. "I had a terrible inferiority complex," Elton explained later. "To change my name helped me get away from it.''

A year later, Elton underwent a further transformation. Busy recording and performing, he began to lose weight. As he got thinner, the clothes he wore became more and more bizarre. He began appearing in unbelievable outfits — silver, star-studded boots, hot pants and purple tights, sunglasses with lights that flashed on and off.

''I've always wanted to walk around in outrageous clothes,'' Elton explained, ''but I couldn't because I was fat. When I lost a lot of weight, that meant I could get into things. Since then, I've always been ostentatiously dressed. I really get a kick out of wearing funny clothes.''

About the same time he began wearing his outrageous outfits, Elton's performances became equally wild. His jumping around actually started accidentally at an outdoor festival in Halifax, Scotland. It was early spring, and the temperature was nearly freezing. Elton began joking with the members of the band about how they could keep warm during their act.

''Hey, you've always been into Jerry Lee Lewis-type acts, haven't you?'' someone asked Elton.

Suddenly he had a brainstorm. ''If I start jumping about, not even caring what I'm doing,'' he said, ''at least I'll keep warm.'' Elton found that besides keeping him warm, jumping around was a lot of fun. And the crowd was enjoying it, too. From then on, it became part of his act. The transformation of Reggie Dwight was complete!

# Elton Conquers

In 1969, Elton John's first album, *Empty Sky,* was released in England. The album contained an entire zoo of psychedelic sound effects: giraffe bellows, lions in the bush and thumping congas, distortion, echo chambers and wind tunnels. The songs were strange and sometimes nightmarish, but they successfully conveyed a mood of utter desolation. *Melody Maker* called *Empty Sky* "a fine debut." But the album sold almost nothing.

The slow sales of *Empty Sky* disappointed Elton and Bernie. But they weren't discouraged. They were already spending every spare moment in the recording studio, working on their next project. When he heard the demos, their friend Steve Brown, who had worked with Elton on *Empty Sky,* suggested that they find a professional arranger for the next album.

At Steve's suggestion, Elton and Bernie went to see Paul Buckmaster, a cello-player who'd become a rock musician. When Buckmaster heard a rough demo of "Your Song," he said he didn't want the job. "It sounds too nice as it is," he said. But eventually he agreed to do the arrangements.

The *Elton John* album was as original as *Empty Sky.* Bernie's lyrics were no less strange and romantic. Again, Elton's melodies and husky voice created an intense mood of loneliness and loss. But rather than a cosmic emptiness, the songs on the *Elton John* album portrayed a loneliness that was human and personal — the brief flickering of love in a hostile world, the relentless passing of time, and, finally, the loss of faith and love with death.

The Elton John album was released in England in May, 1970. Music critics were complimentary. "It's rare to find a person who creates his own form of music," said one. "That's what Elton John has done."

"Heavy intellectual music," declared another critic.

"An album of almost primitive beauty," raved a third.

But once again, sales were slow. The album barely

climbed onto the BBC charts, then slipped right off again. An American company was interested in releasing the record in the United States, but they told Elton he'd have to come over and promote it.

Elton had quit Bluesology to get off the road. He wasn't anxious to start touring again. But it was beginning to look as though he had no choice. Reluctantly, he agreed to make the trip. A concert was scheduled for August 25, 1970, at the Troubador Club in Los Angeles. Two friends, Dee Murray and Nigel Olsson, agreed to back Elton on bass and drums. Although he doubted whether anything would come of the trip, Elton began to look forward to wandering through the fabulous L.A. record stores.

But to Elton's surprise, his American debut was a smashing success. Many of the top music stars were in the audience. The crowd went wild over every song. As Elton started his last number, "Burn Down the Mission," he suddenly noticed one of his rock heroes, Leon Russell, sitting in the front row. Seeing Russell made Elton so nervous, he almost forgot the words. But at the end of the number, Russell was clapping as hard as everyone else. After the concert, he invited Elton to his house for a jam session.

"It was like a schoolboy's fantasies coming true," sighed Elton later, ". . . it was the week of the Million Handshakes."

# Superstar

After his stunning success in Los Angeles, Elton John's records were suddenly in demand both in England

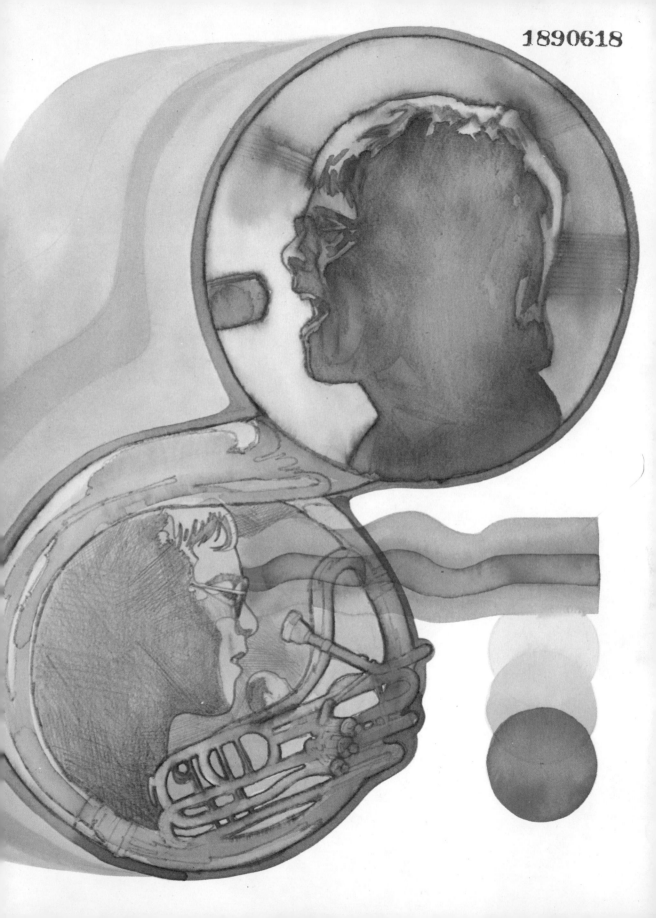

and in America. "*Tumbleweed Connection,*" an album of songs about the American West, was quickly released, followed shortly by *11-17-70,* a recording of a live performance. Elton and Bernie wrote the soundtrack for the movie *Friends,* which was also released as an album.

Suddenly, Elton was caught up in a whirlwind of composing, recording, and performing. "Every time we went into the studio, it was a rush," he remembers. "Two days to go, and he hasn't written the songs yet!" Within six months, Elton had made two major American tours, playing to packed houses in all the major cities. He'd also made a world tour, stopping in the U.S., France, Japan, and Australia. In less than a year, four of Elton John's albums had climbed to the top of the charts, and three had been certified gold, with sales of over a million dollars.

By the end of 1971, the frantic pace was taking its toll. Doctors warned Elton he was on the verge of a nervous breakdown. The strain showed in his 1971 album, *Madman Across the Water.* It proved to be one of his best-selling records, but Elton says now it's the one album he can't bear to hear. "My vocals are appalling," he says, "but that album was made under nightmare conditions." The recording had to be finished in just 10 days, and the pressure got to everyone. At one point, 60 string musicians were waiting at the studio, ready to record; and Paul Buckmaster showed up without having written the score.

After *Madman,* Elton decided that some changes had to be made. He just couldn't accept all the concert bookings he was offered. He would have to slow down. The strain was making him take both the praise and the criticism of the press too much to heart. He was beginning to do what he said he never would — take his music too seriously. It wasn't fun anymore.

Elton was determined that the next album would be different. It would be simpler. The band had gone about as far as they could with Paul Buckmaster's elaborate arrangements. But without the orchestra, they needed a guitar. With no lead guitar, Elton had to be everything — lead instrument, rhythm instrument, and voice. The upshot was that guitarist Davey Johnstone joined Elton, Dee Murphy, and Nigel Olsson to record *Honky Chateau,* an upbeat, happy, simpler album.

To do the recording, the whole group moved into an elegant 16th century French chateau, which had been converted into recording studios. The quiet of the French countryside was both soothing and inspiring. Bernie wrote away furiously in an office upstairs and rushed lyrics down to Elton, who immediately began working out the melodies on the piano. In just three weeks, the songs were written, rehearsed, polished, and recorded.

Though it was done quickly, Elton considers *Honky Chateau* one of their best albums. "You can relate to it on stage," he says. "I knew they wouldn't be able to say, 'Well, it's Elton John and his screechy orchestra'."

## Elton Now

In his latest albums, Elton has been trying to achieve more of a total group sound, rather than that of a soloist with back-up accompaniment. All the publicity he's gotten in the past few years has made Elton increasingly uncomfortable.

He feels the other band members should share the spotlight. "It's not just me," he says. "Okay, I write the songs, and Taupin writes the lyrics; but when we come to record, it's very much an equal thing . . . I'm no better than anyone else." In the next album, *Captain Fantastic,* the group, including Bernie, will be called The Elton John Band.

Elton has a genuine respect for other people and for their individual talents. He doesn't tell the other band members how to play — he trusts their ability and their judgment. Similarly, when he orders his costumes, Elton doesn't tell the designer what to make. "I feel that creative people should be allowed to do what they want without being told," he says.

Elton John believes that any number of performers could be as successful as he is, if only they were given the chance. To help them, Elton has started his own company, Rocket Records. At Rocket, Elton is trying to give unknown but promising artists a fairer deal than they would get from larger companies. Already, Rocket has launched one successful performer, Kiki Dee, who in one recent poll was voted the number one female vocalist in England. "That's nothing particular that *we*'ve done," Elton says. "All we've done is given her the confidence to do it on her own."

Although he thoroughly enjoys his stage act, Elton still considers himself primarily a songwriter, rather than an entertainer. But when he does perform, he's determined to give the audience "a really nice show." He doesn't think people should have to sit through a dull performance where a group just gets up on stage and stands around singing.

Elton likes to surprise his audiences. Lately, his shows have been zanier than ever, with cascades of pianos, mock crocodiles, and hundreds of dancing girls. But that doesn't mean he's not serious about his music. He is a

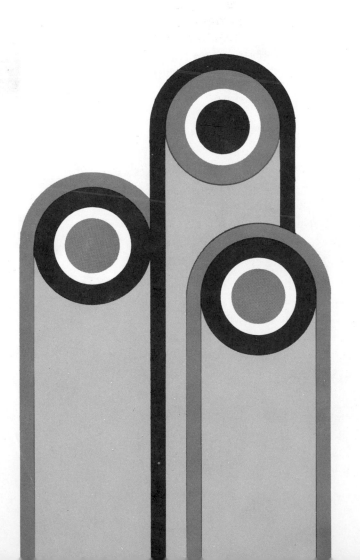

perfectionist who will make 12 or 13 takes of a single track to get things just right. If something turns out badly, he readily owns up to it.

But he will fight for a song he's proud of. In 1971, the Dick James Music Company was objecting to releasing the song "Daniel" as a single, saying it would compete with Elton's top-selling album, *Don't Shoot Me — I'm Only the Piano Player* and his hit single, "Crocodile Rock." But Elton insisted on releasing "Daniel." "It's one of the best songs we've ever written," he said. "I don't care if it's a hit or not. I just want it out."

Elton tries not to let the ecstatic reviews he's been getting affect him. He knows he won't be on top forever, but that doesn't bother him. And it doesn't bother either Elton or Bernie that even the hit songs they write will probably be forgotten in a year's time. "Songs are like pints of milk," Elton says. "You drink one, like it, then want another one."

Now that he's become a superstar, Elton has found that success is not quite as sweet as he expected it to be. He has little time for himself. His telephone is always ringing. Someone always wants him for something. Sometimes Elton finds himself looking back wistfully to the simpler days when he and Bernie stayed at Wimpy's hamburger grill till 4:00 a.m. talking over plans for their albums, too excited to sleep. Now that their dreams have come true, he says, "so much magic has been lost."

The loss of the magic of innocence is the subject of most of the songs on the album, *Goodbye, Yellow Brick Road.* The song "Roy Rogers" sums up the empty feeling one gets on discovering that the Yellow Brick Road doesn't lead to the Emerald City after all: "Sometimes you dream/Sometimes it seems/There's nothing there at all./

You just seem older than yesterday / And you're waiting for tomorrow to call.''

But with the loss of his youthful dreams, Elton has gained a sense of perspective. He's able to stand back and look at life with a sense of humor. The *Yellow Brick Road* album reflects his new maturity. Many of the songs are ironic; and the music has a jazzy, upbeat feel.

Elton considers *Yellow Brick Road* his masterpiece. But he's resisted the temptation to keep on doing his ''Greatest Hits'' all the time, instead of going on to something new. Elton doesn't want to fall into that trap. He intends to keep on improving and progressing.

Elton wants his stage show to keep on changing, as well. He is learning to play the guitar and eventually hopes to play it on stage. He would like to add another keyboard player to the band — perhaps a specialist in organs and mood synthesizers, which he's never quite mastered.

Elton and Bernie feel that the reason they've stayed on top as long as they have in the competitive pop music field is that they can write so many different kinds of songs. Their influences range from classical music to rock 'n roll, from country western to blues. None of their albums sounds the same as any other.

Elton can't predict what the band or their music will be like in a few years — or how he himself might change. ''I could tell you a thousand things today,'' he says, ''and reverse them all tomorrow.'' There's only one thing that's sure, and that is that Elton John will always be involved with music. ''Whatever happens,'' he says, ''I could never do without music . . . music is my life.''

JACKSON FIVE     NEIL DIAMOND
CARLY SIMON     CAROLE KING
BOB DYLAN     DIANA ROSS
JOHN DENVER     THE OSMONDS
THE BEATLES     CHARLIE RICH
ELVIS PRESLEY     ELTON JOHN
JOHNNY CASH     CHICAGO
CHARLEY PRIDE     FRANK SINATRA
ARETHA FRANKLIN     BARBRA STREISAND
ROBERTA FLACK     OLIVIA NEWTON-JOHN
STEVIE WONDER

# Rock'n PopStars